April

Sara Nicholson

The Song Cave

The Song Cave
www.the-song-cave.com

Cover drawing by Emma Steinkraus

Design and layout by Janet Evans-Scanlon

Author photo by Cody-Rose Clevidence

ISBN: 978-1-7372775-9-0
Library of Congress Control Number: 2023931143

FIRST PRINTING

Contents

But I, a poor wretch, have need of everything.

—ST. TERESA OF ÁVILA

What I Said, Where I Said It, and Why

To hear myself say it
To listen to myself saying it to you
Who listen, to them or who
Cares why I said it
That I said it for a reason
Or not, to you or not to you.
When I said it I said it
On the street, by the pier, in a city
On the water.
I said it in the forests
Of America. A little songbird
Who is frightened of the moon
She hears me say it to you
Who listen, I hear her
Who hears me too.
I don't think she listens
When I say it.
She sings to us the vowels
In a sequence—ee, ah, oo, ay; ee, ah, oo, ay.
Did Helen say it to Clytemnestra.
Did Laura Riding
Overhear her say it to me.
I believe what I hear
In dreams, the people who speak

From inside me in dreams
Who whisper to me
The whys and hows of saying
It to you. I can't believe
I said it to you.
Are there any good poems
About saying it.
If you find one let me know.

Weather Talk

Something about the music grief is
Either prey to or heir to
Falls flat, the same way art is
Subject to its objects: larks & light
On a table, the pink green
Breezes through all August long.
I know the things I know
Nothing about might be things
Worth knowing. Weather
Maps, for example, or how to read
The Zodiac, the language of
Dreams. I don't know how to write
About the world, what art says
Vis-à-vis the dark & bright
Ocean; why black, orange, blue,
And copper metaphorically
Flower and fruit. I'd like to write
An elegy in verse or prose
But I've never been able to read
Music, refuse to sing or sign
My name. I know things
Aren't quite so simple, that partly
Cloudy days prefigure nights
Without rain, rain the sun,

The sun the limits of my world
And I, the plural form
Predominant in November,
December, January, calendrical
Time, pain, grief, joy, energy
And entropy, all the state
Flowers: red, gold, purple, white.

Spain

Having never been to Spain
I left for it, as one who
Hazards faith in vagueness. The rose
Shrieks each autumn, dies
Tragically. The pomegranate, too,
Has nothing of interest to say.
All fruit trees flower
But in Spain, they *florecen*—minor
Differences of sounds like these
The traveler must learn.
One must occasionally allow oneself
Bourgeois imaginings
As of wine flights by the sea
Or the carpeted staircases
Of castles, renovated by the state.
I am a very rich woman
Who winters in Tenerife, the Spanish crown
Seeks my guidance on all matters
Tenerife-related. I feel
Melancholy when it snows
Over the Atlantic, from the window
Of my castillo. Mere presence
With no cause for concern
My life is lived

For me by others, portioned out
In intervals of rest and music
(It should be obvious
By now that I have many servants.
All are well paid).
The white buildings of Cádiz
Communicate in pictures other truths
Than those intended.
The act of reading
Has become for me a form
Of blunt force trauma to the head.
Thus was I persuaded
To enter this sanitorium
Where beneath the well-clipped ilex
Acorn-fed swine roam wild
Until the peasants slaughter them
For their sweet flesh, rumored
To have healing properties—I am here
For my health, trusting
That the Mediterranean will work
Its slow miracle on the brain. I was born
For convalescence, the daughter
Of Doña Maria, Baronesa.
Each September
I leave a flower on her grave.

The Archetype

Even Cézanne painted her, naked of course,
reclining on a chair. The mythical
Leda, mother of Helen, raped by a metamorphosed
Zeus in the guise of a swan.
She faces front, and we can almost see
everything—the hips, the uneven
Breasts, the nipples that echo her blush-pink
knees and cheeks, but not
Her vulva, as it's cloaked by a twisted
piece of cloth. She looks bored.
Unlike Delacroix's Leda, who appears to be choking
the neck of the swan, her back
Facing us, hiding from view her naughtier
bits which, however, I think,
The swan can still see. Cézanne's Zeus
bites Leda's wrist. Or maybe he's
Shaking her awake? Like the way Yeats's bird
pecks at her, grabs her "nape"
In his "bill" in mid-air; this is a sonnet
and by the volta we learn
Her vagina is Troy. I don't like the modern
paintings of her story. I prefer
Those Renaissance Ledas, plopped in
landscapes rich in Arcadian

Cliché—chasms, mountains, and clumps
of woods; palazzi with views of
The Florentine hills. Michaelangelo painted them
fucking. Correggio, too, who stuffs
His canvas with babies and angels, lyres,
flutes, swans, and naked ladies
Who bear witness to the mytho-erotic act.
But Da Vinci's Leda forgoes
The sex, depicts instead the hatchlings
Castor and Pollux, Helen
and Clytemnestra, sons and daughters of
Zeus who bears the Aegis,
Her fledgling brood, all pudgy, balding,
and bandy-legged, tenderly
Dwarfed by their shells. Still others chose
to depict her inside, to move from
The public to the private sphere, as in Veronese's
Leda, where we, the voyeur,
Watch the two embrace, she with a hand
at the base of his tail, he sticking
His beak in her mouth. She's naked, apart from
her jewelry. The boudoir's
Draped in velvet, her hair bedewed
with pearls. We are meant
To be titillated—this is adultery, after all,
however grotesque—so it's ok
If you feel a frisson as you eavesdrop
on the primal scene.

My favorite Leda is also *en couchant*, splayed
wide before divinity, so wide
We get an unobstructed view of her
vagina while the swan
Peers into it, transfixed as by the void of
archaic memory. Call it
The ornithological gaze. This Leda
has no author, is attributed
to François Boucher, master of the Rococo
nude, the plump and idle
Venus on a chaise. Each of the above
mentioned artists paints
The sex as consensual, as seduction rather than
rape. Therefore Leda's story
Is the story of interpretation itself
in every possible style—
There are Pre-Raphaelite Ledas, cubist,
surrealist and neoclassical
Ones. You can find her in miniature
and on the decorative
Lids of snuffboxes, in mosaic and frieze.
Yet Twombly's is the only Leda
To eschew both nudity and naivete. Its subject
is, we might say, movement
Itself—the flapping wings, the shock and
clash, the chaos and the strife.
Crazy brushstrokes, lines and dripping paint
suggest feathers, maybe

Blood, too. He has obviously painted
a rape. I was inspired
By my research to look up YouTube
videos of swans mating and
As you might've guessed, swan sex is difficult
to watch—the male grabs
The female's neck, holds her head
underwater for so long
She occasionally drowns. A user named
Geof commented "Um there
Bangin" and not to kink-shame the natural
but with Mr.Bright68 I'd have
To agree: "This is not normal not love."
The Old Masters, I'm shocked
Not one of them ever chose to paint
the egg-laying, or to pair her
With another of those mythical feminine
archetypes—the Fates and Furies,
The loathly lady, a huntress or gorgon
with snakes for hair. I'd like
To see Leda in Heaven, or like Persephone
rule death, restore flowers
To usher in Spring. To see her wander
like Odysseus to Circe's
Island, wave at Scylla and Charybdis
on her way to Hell.
She might have murdered Tyndareus,
her husband, a King of Sparta.

Like Medea, she could've smashed her eggs.
    The oldest works of art
To depict Leda's story—a Greek amphora
    now in Los Angeles, a fresco
In Pompeii—show her kissing and fucking
    the swan, respectively. In one
She stares right at us, from the ruins
    of a Roman bedroom. In one
She is naked, but in the other, clothed.

Lines Heard

I absent myself from fate
A little too often, snowdrops
Spring upon us yet again
In colors dripped on the grass
Which is dead, whoever'd
Speak the picture into being
Another non sequitur the night
Falls next to, follows after
For me, it is part of that magic
Riders see from a train
Row houses, kids and flowers
Amtrak's Northeast Corridor
Frames, makes art from
The linnet seed, cadmium white
Dots the earth and trees withdraw
In ever smaller numbers
Because none of this hurts
The earth itself because it too
Lilts uglily, taxes the woods
All systems depend on
The end of systematization
In a handful of snow we spring
Upon each other, collect
A surcharge on the winter air

Who spends a lifetime
Accumulating warmth for us
Who are a people in transit
Toward a destination
We don't know, that is to say
I would begin to sing it
For you, I'd tell the story
End-stopped by snow, the poem
Of a world without pain
We are capable of imagining
A better ending for it
Disquiets the sea with rain

Nut

It must be nice to own
A strong feeling.
To walk about the towns and fields of Earth
A man of taste, a woman
Who lacks confidence
In the public and its institutions
And is therefore serious
About art. About line and color
I feel very little.
Textures make me nervous:
The trunks of trees,
The flesh of the octopus, its suckers,
Hair and horns.
What is it about the abstract
Words for feelings that bothers me? Is it
The dailiness of ecstasy
Or the ecstasy of dailiness?
Rage and integrity, why do they stun?
The plastic tub of bluets
In my neighbor's backyard
Embarrasses me.
Bodies embarrass me, as does the soul
When aflame, with grief or dolor.
A woodcut of the Magdalen,

Doughty and rough-hewn.
Though easily put off by feelings
I am not ashamed
Of my embarrassment. It is natural
To be petty about beauty,
To want to hold it in your hand
With purpose, and reduce it
To the size of a nut.
Trees in poems, especially trees
In my own poems
I am not ashamed to admit
Embarrass me.
It must be nice to live among them
Under a clear, blue sky
In October, my trees
Full of laughter and weeping,
Plagued by an idiom.
I do not envy them Poetry. Oh Lord
They can have it.

To the Committee

The houses are blue, cream, and white.
That one is painted Miami
Dolphins colors. Orange & aqua
with white trim.
The snow is sparkly.
The sky is gray.
A squirrel is saying *brick brick*
To the cat.
I have an exemplary record of service
At the University level.
A wreath
Of plastic berries.
A White Claw and a Natty
Daddy in the snow.
Thank you
For your consideration.
I look forward to hearing from you.

A Crown for Iris

for Hannah Brooks-Motl

"There is no beyond, there is only here,
The infinitely small, infinitely
Great, and utterly demanding present."
So says a character in an Iris
Murdoch novel, although I get a whiff
Of authorial interjection here,
An axiom, all puzzle without proof,
As if Murdoch herself is affirming
Reality over the void, the here
And now above some hypothetical
Eternity. The paradox I seek's
Above all else an ever-present link
To the past: Wordsworthian daffodils
Ad infinitum, nightingales in Keats.

Literary birds *ad infinitum*
Along with flowers, poetry's bad faith.
I don't believe in God and yet I do
Believe in ∞, the power
Of the present tense, particularly
To forfeit myth and vanish the divine
Motif fire is, to siphon off the sea.
But what is limitless is limited
By our ability to conceive of
Unbounded space. Conceptualizing
The infinite requires us to think
Differently, to find what Murdoch found
Extraordinary about the present:
The poetry of ordinary life.

The ordinary life of poetry's
Both intimate and infinite. A song
Celan said must be sung "beyond / mankind"
To mourn mankind, a philosophical
Problem at the root of poetry. But
∞ in pure mathematics
Can be counted and so my idea of
Poetry as unquantifiable
Grief falls apart, an infinite set
The alphabet gave birth to, goddess-like,
For all mankind to sing beyond & as
Radii of the elegiac: the I
Who speaks, the you who hears, the we who mourn
The Alpha and Omega, A to Z.

A to Z, the end and the beginning
Of the world, they circle back and in so
Circling, return us to the present:
"The infinitely small, infinitely
Great, and utterly demanding present."
The beauty of the immaterial
Material, is that what Murdoch meant
Us to notice? The loco-descriptive
Power of poetry, seasonally
Affective? October's trompe l'œil effects?
No. I find the present tense the perfect
Symbol of ∞ since both are
Continuous, portions of the sacred
Everyday I go to sleep with, wake to find.

I wake up early nearly every day
Thinking of ∞. The cosmos
And the laws of quantum particles, lines
Of poetry, irrational numbers
Of birds. I live my life in thrall to it
Yet court the finite, pray the hyperreal
Adds brevity to the equation, proof
The infinitesimal is infinite.
I wake up early nearly every day
Imagining ∞ a song.
I'm not the first to notice the divine
Prerogative of the artist, akin
To God since both invent a universe
Out of nothing, a new cosmology.

The universe, apropos of nothing
Exists and thrives, the same way poetry
Parallels music's ability to
Unify the abstract and the concrete,
The general with the particular.
From one leaf, a tree; from one tree, ideas
Of the natural and by logical
Extension the unnatural: man-made
Disasters, fires, spills, and urban sprawl.
The rising cost of lumber. The rising
Cost of housing. The problems are nearly
Infinite, so many that it would take
A googolplex of Aeolian harps
To quantify the lyric, count the grief.

To tally grief, first quantify the lyric
And add to the poetic the idea
Of infinitely many worlds, plus one
In which we live our lives, the present tense.
For every n an $n+1$. For each
And every bird, another bird, and then
Another, until the number of birds
Approaches ∞ and the Earth
Itself grows wings, and migrates to a star
Far from our own. "I close my eyes and see
A flock of birds," an inconceivable
Number, Borges writes. "Ergo, God exists."
If divinity is ordinary
There is only here, there is no beyond.

Song

potato masher, tin foil, rubber
spatula, a dog doing
its business on
the Cadman Plaza locust
tree half-heartedly if
again & again
& again, stinging witch
hazel, a rattlesnake
plant next to peacock prayer
plants in a window, O
spatula, O chicken-
of-the-woods
with wine, tweezers, the idea
of the soul as
immortal, a puff of air,
a flame, I
turn to them all,
to each of them in turn
I turn, O toothbrush, woolly old
peacoat on a nail

Plants in a Window

Some such disarray, as in a Balthasar
van der Ast painting of *Semper*
augustus, the parti-flamed
"tulip of the rich," or better yet a Jane
Freilicher, all bouquet splash
and Bonnard-y light cherry-picked
from the real. I'm alive
to the risk such beauty brings
to the problem of design, as in de Chirico
still lifes, where busts and flagons
zig-zag off the curvilinear
or in Chardin, that genius of the humble
kitchen scene: apples and pears
plus flambeaux, crockery, and pussy
frisking a hare, a rustic loaf.
A table top "ensnar'd with flow'rs"
and contrapposto, à la Breughel the Elder.
The macro and the micro-
scopic detail, unifying the various
parts of a world: the globes
in Holbein's *Ambassadors*; peaches
by contrast, in a basket or bowl.

Ode

There are no secrets
In Poetryland
A little cloud or two
The sun rhymes
Open, scans
Brazenly
The sky for a welt
This poem goes out
To the man
Who told E. she writes
"Like a man"
You might know him
You can do it
To literally anything
Rilke made love
To angels
Leopardi sought
His little hill in a dream
A red barn
A house painted
Corn or grain
Yellow
A candle above
The marriage bed

The hydrangea
Solidly middle class
Can I say
Winter is pretty
Without reference
To the cold
The illusion of depth
In landscapes
Do I appear
By chance to know
How best to wield the violet
We have MFAs
In wielding the violet
A whisper network
Like no other
Marching through
Harsh winds
A whole chunk of ice
On the state
Flower of New Jersey
DNA everywhere

Utopia

after Michael Burkard

Are you mad at me?
Don't be. I know I can be
Difficult. The perfect word
Is hard to find, syntax
Can be difficult to parse, it's true.
And although there are those who find
Difficulty a virtue, madness too,
I aim to simplify
My loss, ambition, rage and joy
Into a single word
And speak it to you, Love,
As I've been speaking all along
Of hardship and crisis, the dream
Of utopia, a word only
Visible by grace of the dark.

The Burden

I don't know the Latin names of flowers.
I know that there are cities wherein stars

Will labor to appear in bursts of *as*
Or *under*, will command the color green

To work with *from* or *of* or *in* in staves
And paragraphs, will demarcate the limits

Of the sky. I recognize the colors
Of acacia from paintings and poems.

I know a high wind carries rhyme *across*
The ocean. That smoke, it coaxes signals

From the fire. What words you speak I too
Have spoken of: of *of*, the turning *back*,

The opening *beyond* and *up above* us,
The movement *forward* and the reasoning

Behind. I know that the horizon falls *out*
Of perspective, that toward music the sea

Will harken *back* and find in language
No beauty save impermanence, a minor awe.

Everyone's Poem

Life is pleasant. Paradise too
Dry or wet. Scarcity's
A nail driven through the concrete
Slab in a garden, soon to be
Overcome by weeds, wildfire

Particles in the air. And so I
Willed for myself a life
Apart from you, one in which
Apricots fell freely to all
Who would eat them, no thirst

For money, the burnished coin
Of my rage. Yet all along
We were helping them to divide
Each week into units, wages
Exchanged for time or time's

Pure potential, forms of play
Set apart from the hourly
Relation of one thing to all
Others, vexed by the spark
From which our sense of time

Derives. It shouldn't come
As a shock to you, that I myself

Thrive on disbelief even as I
Queue up a song, am what isn't
Right with the world, in other

Words, everything. How I long
To live, as angels do, in utter
Obedience to a power, whose law
Provokes no rumor of music
Favoring the hush that follows

A shift of tense or pronoun
On cool May mornings, likely
Milder than the present
Climate crisis should permit.
I was in New York, I think

It was colder than it should be
Anywhere, a certain time of year
My scant affinity for rain
Misread, so that I could tell you
Writing it takes synthesizing

Everyone, everything and what
Each word means to you
Laid bare within the sentence
Leaves drying on the black top
Loosely iambic, wet with ash

Irrespective of how we define
A season, a series of hours

Distributed equally, as—as one
Overburdened by heat or snow—
I always found myself

Unprepared for it, lacking the right
Clothes, the so-to-speak right
To imagine a door opening onto
A field of sun-burnt grasses
And white lilac, painfully sincere

Light spilling back into April
Privacy, all adjective minus
The gerund, obscuring my motives,
Ceasing to harbor the disparate
Business of stars along my route.

A Link to the Past

Take hold of shield and buckler —PSALM 35

My triumph was assured so long as
I labored to complete my tasks.
I rode my avatar's horse
From meadow to lake, slung nuts
Dropped by an ancient
Spirit in the form of a tree
At my enemies, whose near-constant presence
Made the task of slaying
All of them impossible, inevitably leading
Me to question the ontology
Of such a world, one in which my death
Meant little since I found myself
Resurrected an infinite
Number of times, brought back
To where I'd begun
My quest, only to combat
More of my enemies who themselves
Never died, but instead dissolved
Painlessly, it seemed to me,
Into the earth. The fairy forest's
Mercantile economy
Ensured that I spent much of my time
Slashing the hedges for coins

To exchange for goods
That promised to advance me
In my quest, such as health-giving potions
Or heavy, unstylish boots
Which would allow me to walk
Undetected at the bottom of the sea.
I was permitted to slaughter
My enemies, but not the peaceful
Inhabitants of the villages I came across
Though I tried many times
Many, many times
To stab them. I was permitted
To hurt chickens, which I did do
Though I then risked being
Subsequently attacked and killed
By the rest of the flock, which I was.
My boomerang was taken
From me when I reached maturity
By performing a song
On the dais of a temple's steps
But now that I'm an adult
My tasks are more difficult.
I must balance
Many of these tasks at once
And learn the more complicated
Songs, how to navigate
My fear of failure

In the face of such dangers.
Worst of all my quest
Is interrupted day and night by others
Who call on me to serve
Their needs.

Astrology and the Death Drive

after Jennifer Moxley

Some tally stars, forgetful to appoint
Others the task of marking beat or stress.
Others, tasked with possibility, click
The link embedded in an article
On stars, their origin in wick and flame
An ode to what's possible, an idea.
Love's orbit faltered, and I lost my way
In a dark wood, the *selva oscura*
In which birds erase the boorish heart of
All discourse with their song, identical
To the infinite or finite, never
Both. Overrun with water, floods and rains,
And with anemone, little *pense-bêtes*
Of spring, we await a freer syntax
Than English allows, recycle language
On dying land the astrological
Signs never reference, the pastoral
Of capital, in which flowers and stars
Are likewise monetized, shared across all
Platforms, liked, inevitably taken
Out of context, gone viral, now data
For content-driven marketers, renamed
And reinvested, trending globally,

Exalted by the poetry of old
Lacedaemon, Persia, Troy. Venus'
Locus, her scallop-shell barque, plummets
Pink-veined into the sea. Jupiter ebbs
With the market while its ion-fed moons,
Like Benjamin's Angel of History,
Brave fire, war with centuries-old storms.
Neptune in Leo, the mechanical
Orgy of mythos and star, travels south
This time of year, shedding chlorophyll-hued
Gas on Cassiopeia, her daughter
Still chained to the rock; then it veers
Left beyond Virgo, occults Saturn,
To dissolve with the elliptical path
Of the sun. None of this means anything,
Is merely an excuse to satisfy
A human need for order, the sublime.
My horoscope says in the year to come
I'll wander in, ferried by candlelight,
Awaiting the millennium, eager
For Lucifer to quicken those who sleep.
I'll survey morning, inquire after
Lark or oak as archetype of people
Not on social media, those whom fate
Has left behind, in privacy, to pluck
Clarity from the sentence, wit from time.
Those who consent, without reservation.
Wary of faith, but by devotion cursed.

Nature Is Art

Despair desires despair; desire
Despairs of desiring. Despair despairs
Of ever again desiring to desire
Despair, while desire desires
A form: a garden in the orthodox
Narrative, flowering *ex nihilo*
From April to October in the *Roman
De la Rose*, the Belle Epoque.
But what would happen if desire
Abandoned desire, desiring
In lieu of desire despair, an elegy
That would suffice to burn
The garden down? It was desire
Despair desired until desire
Fell into despair, built a replica
Of the garden it had only just
Yesterday burned: a copy of a copy
Now lost, complete with fake
Flowers. Not a fire, but gold leaf.

The Goatherd and the Saint

Immiseration is a beautiful
Word. A woman
On her phone
Next to *The Polish Rider*
Playing Candy Crush.
I read the bright
Red of the rider's leg and hat
In conversation with
A line of buttons
Down the front of his fur
Cloak. The mystery
Of portraiture
Without context, it adds
Narrative to
The phenomenal
Details: are those tears
In the horse's eye?
Why the knee
At the painting's center?
I understand his
Need for a hammer but
Why the jaunty
Angle of his grasp?
Best to remain

Oblivious of the Fragonards
In the next room over
At the Frick
The Gilded Age
Mansion on the Upper
East Side. Love's pursuit
Is here depicted as
The triumph
Of patriarchal folly
Wherein boys and girls are
Addled by the sylvan
Drapery, proffer
Nosegays as a heartfelt
Caveat to a regime
On the brink of
Revolution. The avant
Garde "pleasure
Pavilion" for which
The Fragonards were long ago
Commissioned, imagine
Yourself inside it.
Assaulted by
The proto-Romantic sublime
You wait hours to slip
A note to me
Who is either a servant or
A knave in silks.
A tearful

Scene beside a brook
Reaps from on high a *Hark! Hark!*
But there is a world
Outside of art
And love is not just
Froth and curls.
Besides as someone who
Has studied both
Anatomy and poetry
I'd have to say
Love's seat
Within the body is
Not the heart, but the lymph
A fluid that purifies
And destroys all
Toxins, debris, and germs.
The Frick Bellini
St. Francis in the Desert
I'm in love
With the way it seems to frown
Above the objets d'art
Arrayed about
The hall, stripping the last
Veneer of sentiment
From the neo-baroque flowering
Of these interiors,
The desert's various blues
Made all the more

Austere by
Such a contrast.
Paroxysm is a beautiful
Word. As in what
Francis experiences
Late in the day,
A vision
And its attendant spirits,
Terror and ecstasy,
Which soon, upon his death
A few years later
Will vanish but still haunt
The craquelure.
Happy, well-
Educated, you find yourself
Waylaid by the forms
The sacred takes:
A donkey and heron,
A rabbit
Popping its head out
Beneath Francis's right hand,
A pair of sandals,
A skull and prayer book
Resting on a desk.
Is it possible
Zion's proverbs have
Backfired, that every bird has
Wandered wildly out of

The frame toward
A quorum
We can't join?
Notice the little pinpricks
Of his stigmata
The only
Red among the vast
Lascaux-like effects of shade,
The dark green,
Peaches and periwinkles
The artist chose for
His palette.
I admit
I'm afraid to look at
St. Francis's eye, so as to avoid
A potential reflection
Of the seraph that
So affixed his gaze
He remains
Centuries later trapped
Within the zeal of its purview.
I could go on
But the saint is not
My focus here.
Rather, the world
He's escaped from is, a bridge
Toward the citadel
In the top-left

Corner and the people
Who must surely live there,
The far-off palaces
That crown
The deep blue hills.
A goatherd and his flock
Adds a touch of
Pathos to the overall
Effect. Work
Without pay, what remains
Of the many-headed
Hydra that is
The medieval worldview
The half-starved
Michaelmas daisy, St. John's wort
Fainting in the loggia,
The vines that sever Francis
From the rocks
And grow
Atop the grotto
That is his sacristy.
Henry Clay Frick, a lifelong
Enemy of labor
Was also a lifelong
Lover of art.
No one except
The goatherd and the saint
Is visible to us

Which begs
The question, who lives
In that palace?
Who plows their fields?
Consider
The reproductive labor
Art demands
From each of us
In turn, who exist to house
Bellinis the world over
And live
In a state of anxious
Reckoning with
Our complicity, New York
Money laundered
By the spirit of the Old
Master paintings
I paid $22
To see. I'm in love
With the donkey at the edge
Of the cliff, the heron
Beside him.
They must have a place
Within the symbolic
Universe of
Bellini's painting,
An allegory of the sacred
Set in a desert

Paradox, all crag and rock
Strata, pointy edges
Which embrace
Water as well, a miraculous
Surplus of flora.
I can relate
To the awkwardness
Of the donkey's
Backbone, the poignancy
Of his stance:
Wobbly, knock-kneed
But strapping, a scarcely
Noticeable smile
On his face.
I want to watch him feed
On something
Delicious, an apple
Or an ear of wheat, nuzzle
Flax from the granary.
My donkey, I think
He is happy.
I can almost hear him
Clip-clopping over the rocks.
The private parts
Of marriage,
The wet
End of a cigarette
As tender as

Anything really:
The painting's remarkable
Lack of birds, apart
From the heron.
Bellini's signature
On a ragged
Scrap of parchment
In the wind.

April

It can be nice, some days
To sit down and think.
Fresh air is good.
Matter in variety is good
For the body.
A little pepper on the biscuit, not
Too much onion, just a slice.
The sea is calm tonight.
I sought a theme and sought for it in vain.
I'm tired. The wind is blowing
Only just.
The wind is good
And so am I
Bored with desiring, exchanging ticket
For ticket, sail for sail.
The snow is good
And the rain.

To C.

When you wrote "Un coeur en hiver"
When I listened to you read it
A little lyric poem
Not set to music but invoking music's name
When you insisted on using
A name that was not your own
But was of you nonetheless
I was already in love
With you, had been for so long
That I became a person
Of the world, obsessed by prosodies
I couldn't yet break down
But heard everywhere
Around me, in you, of us, the heart
Of winter in your poem.
A line from a song, maybe "Ave Maria"
To measure our distances with.
A paradise that is by nature
Material, it's where
I make my home. I'm not American
In the same way you are. Just so, the nightingale
Was never a lover
Of knowledge in the old-time sense.
When I went to school

To learn the words
That no one ever writes or speaks
When I learned the big words
Like primogeniture, eschatology, and love
I became a person
Aghast at midnight, its sublimity
The vainglory of poets
On Facebook, in Brooklyn or L.A.
I became a person who grew to hate
The sweet flower of April,
The red-and-white one. The purposes
Of meteors and stars.
I listened to a maiden's prayer
Made many centuries ago.
I became a person
Forever cursed to discourse on beauty
In front of nobody on earth
But you.

Lives of the Saints

Spring–Summer 2020

I like some things *because* I don't like others. Rejection is affirmation. And affirmation is necessary for living well.

o

The importance of contrast. Monks and nuns, hermits and feral children: in wildness, we find a critique of civilization and in solitude, a critique of society. The anchoress bricks herself into her cell, the prophet runs away to the desert. They offer the rest of us a precious gift: the gift of reflection. Light and shadow. Poetry and prose.

o

Saints and poets have always weaponized their humility. The lower they sink, the more arrogantly and egotistically they rise above us. In the *Convivio*, Dante compares himself to a dog. He sits under a celestial banquet table, hungry for the scraps that fall from the plates of the angels. This is what I mean by arrogant humility: yes, he's a dog, but at least he's welcome at the feast.

o

The earthworms of North America came originally from Europe, brought here unknowingly by early settlers. They have since founded their own empire—at over five hundred years old, longer than that of the Han Dynasty or Rome—comprised of vast networks of tunnels, billions upon billions of miles in length. Yet worms are humble creatures: they crawl through the mud, are eaten by birds, get stepped on. From them, we learn the power of humility.

o

Water, too. The littlest tide pools host whole ecosystems. A dribble or ooze, given time, will carve a canyon in the rock. If Niagara Falls could speak it would say, in the words of the great diarist Jules Renard, "I very humbly confess my pride."

o

The odds overwhelmingly favor it: your life is not interesting. Why, then, do you write about yourself?

o

All artists think their friends are geniuses. But none of us are special. Our friends are just as unremarkable as the rest of our contemporaries whom we, thinking back to our own group, despise.

o

A friend once told me he thinks poets should be paid the same as fiction writers. This is backward. We should instead pay fiction writers the way poets are paid: very little, infrequently, mostly not at all. Then, there would be no need for agents, major publishing houses, publicity teams, marketing campaigns, spreadsheets of potential sales figures, advance praise (lies), copyrights, contracts, query letters, media kits, press kits, personal websites, professionalization of all kinds. Alternatively, we should pay both poets and fiction writers (along with nurses, teachers, maids, mothers, retail clerks, and sex workers) the same as the President of the United States.

o

Find an obscure subject and learn everything you can about it. Tell no one.

o

Strive to observe the world in ways no one else can or would want to. Sylvia Townsend Warner: "The wind of evening ruffled the pages over, and presently an enterprising spider began to march across the fifth chapter of Deuteronomy. If it had been an ordinary book, he would most probably have gone down the tunnel at the back; but as it was a Bible, and he an insect of character, he essayed the overland route."

o

As the parasite *Toxoplasma gondii* rewires rats' brains, attracting them to the scent of their predators, housecats, so the internet brings together poets from all over the country, that they might tear each other to pieces.

o

Those who hesitate to speak, who choose to maintain what Horace calls a "holy silence," should be the first to open their mouths. This is as true of parties as it is in politics.

o

In the 1890s, a man released into Central Park all the birds from Shakespeare's plays: sparrows and bullfinches, wrens and nightingales and skylarks. I love the frivolity, the childish and impossible whimsy, of his idea. Of course it failed, and European starlings, which he introduced to this continent, devastate native species, destroy crops and orchards every year, and have even crashed planes. The lesson here is simple: only the fruit of our actions counts.

○

Poetry is like a pandemic. A global phenomenon, it spreads easily. It can feel, for the writer, like an affliction. It is hated. It has been known to kill.

○

What we call expertise is more akin to myopia than to keen eyesight. You wouldn't compliment the vision of someone who could see one object clearly and all others blurred. Scholars enrich their knowledge of one subject at the cost of impoverishing their knowledge of a hundred others.

○

In the garden of literature, there is a broken obelisk. It's hidden away, surrounded by thorns. To find it, you must first walk past fountains and statues, woods and arbors, grottoes and budding wildflower meadows. It's difficult to read the inscription on the obelisk because of all the cracks and chips. It is dedicated to the Poetry Foundation, the Academy of American Poets, the Poetry Society of America, the National Book Critics Circle, and the MacArthur Foundation.

○

If I contradict myself, embracing what I claim to despise, attribute this to my humanity. One can't escape one's nature. If I were a dog I too would eat excrement, then roll over to have my belly scratched.

○

The more I learn about something, the more clearly I learn how little I actually know about it. I can't say, in all honesty, that I know how to write. I'm still learning.

○

I want to read poems the way monks read scripture, to practice what is called *lectio divina* ("divine reading"). It's a slow process, like building a fire with wet wood. It requires focus of a radically laborious kind. You might argue that not many poems demand such attention, that this is an unfashionable or even elitist thing to do, and you'd be right of course, but nevertheless, whoever you are—I write for the divine reader in you.

○

We sustain ourselves with books. Some we swallow quickly; others, tougher or richer, we chew. Without our prompting, they make their way through the maze of our interior and the majority of what we take in, we expel. Only the essential nutrients remain.

○

I pick a book off the shelf with my eyes closed, open to a page at random, point to a line, and read: "And he was pursued by the scent of the heliotrope, in twilight that was the same wan mauve as the tiny flower."

○

Cats teach virtue: pleasure without remorse, self-care without vanity, play with a purpose, will in excess. They don't care what anyone thinks of them, apart from the one or two people they love. They have dreams.

○

Poets teach vice: remorse without pleasure, vanity without self-care, purposeless play. They care deeply, to the point of private torment, what strangers think of them. Yet they, too, have dreams.

o

On self-sufficiency. The critic and the poet, the ornithologist and the bird. Tell me, which of these are complete in and of themselves?

o

Optimists are right to pity pessimists their unhappiness. So, too, have pessimists a right to pity optimists their stupidity. The only way to bridge the gap between the two—to be both stupid and despairing—is to fall in love.

o

The fiercest animals are mothers. They starve, they suffer, they attack and they kill to protect their babies. They're often, within species, the most dangerous to encounter in the wild. By analogy: the fiercest poets are mothers.

o

Teaching is difficult. It requires that you bare a piece of your soul to strangers. No wonder, then, that every single day the teacher's soul is violated, spit on, laughed at, trampled underfoot. The trick is to think of these violations as a gift.

o

Conviction, enthusiasm, passion, self-sacrifice, love without reservation, disregard for convention, generosity in abundance—in short, saintliness—would not get one very far today. In the Middle Ages, women were venerated for all sorts of acts which, today, would result in their commitment to an asylum: for stabbing their eyes out (St.

Lucy), for self-starvation (St. Catherine), for eating the scabs and pus of the poor (St. Angela of Foligno), for living for years in a box (Christina of Markyate), for collecting in jars pieces of their own rotting flesh (St. Lidwina). Rather than condemn theirs as a barbarous age, we should instead reflect upon our own.

O

The perfect metaphor for the relationship of critics to poets: vampires. The critic feeds on the poet's soul's nutritive essence. The victim, in turn, hopes for eternal life.

O

A good book made entirely of bad poems. Or the reverse, a bad book of all good poems. A manifesto that makes no demands, a treatise without ideas. A travel guide to imaginary places with intricate pull-out maps of fake cities and glossaries of words in invented languages. Literary hoaxes. Reviews of books that don't exist.

O

If the arts were a city: drama, the Fire Department; philosophy, Sanitation; landscape painting, Parks and Recreation. If the arts were government organs: music, the Department of Energy; poetry, the Department of the Interior.

O

On self-sufficiency. We write because of the little dramas, the interior ones. This is the reason prayer exists, and poetry too: the fantasy of redemption and the illusion of an audience.

O

The spirit of an institution: a contradiction in terms. If the spirit were an institution, how each of us would compromise ourselves, taming what by nature should be wild. We would produce, for the imagination, a strategic plan. We would draft bylaws. The only way forward is revolution: burn the institution of the spirit to the ground, and build something new.

o

There are people who feel the weight of history. Of colossal suffering, atrocity piled on atrocity. This feeling manifests as a deep misanthropy, but also as a love for people beyond anything I've ever seen. They, with all their heart, wish for a meteor to crash into Earth. They also care deeply for their friends, and would protect them until the moment the meteor crashes.

o

Sometimes I feel that I have so much to give, but no one to give it to. In reality I have nothing to give, and anyone can have it.

o

The women of Lemnos. Clytemnestra. Judith. Lizzie Borden. Medea. I love all of you. The Danaïdes.

o

What's most astonishing about Christina the Astonishing is that she is not, technically speaking, a saint. She jumped into fires, let dogs bite her, slept in tombs, and tossed herself into waterwheels until her arms and legs were broken. The wounds she suffered healed instantly. An otherworldly hum, some claimed, seemed to issue from inside her.

She often levitated, so the story goes, to avoid the smell of her fellow parishioners' sins.

○

Religion and art. Two moons orbiting the same planet. Occasionally the moons' paths cross, but the laws of physics ensure the two maintain a proper distance.

○

On self-sufficiency. A man was invited by the stonecutters' guild to work in a faraway quarry. He was lonely when he got there, knowing no one. Though the other stonecutters lived in cabins not too far from his, none would befriend him. So he spent his days quietly, cutting his stone. After years of solitude, of resentment and bitterness at his fellow workers, he realized the blessing that fate had conferred: he had been spared the monotony of their company. And so he worked, and was at peace.

○

Better to live like a crab under a rock than to expose oneself to the open air and risk being eaten by seabirds. In time, you'll grow comfortable under the rock that crushes you.

○

Writing is like walking through a city. You pass an outdoor market. There are bowls and scarves and necklaces, fruit you've never heard of, tiny figures carved from wood. The sun is bright. An old woman is cracking nuts. You touch everything, willfully, lazily, but buy nothing. How are you going to spend your day?

○

St. Wilgefortis, patron of facial hair and abused women, did what she had to do. To avoid an arranged marriage, she prayed to God for help and thereupon grew a beard. Her would-be husband rejected her. Her father, the king, had her crucified for disobedience. In art she is depicted crucified and bearded, dressed in a flowing silk gown. Wives for centuries have prayed to Wilgefortis to take their husbands away from them.

o

On self-sufficiency. After escaping captivity, Christina the Astonishing survived alone in the forest for over two months. What did she eat? According to legend, she prayed to Heaven for food, then looked down to find that "her dry virginal breasts were dripping sweet milk against all the laws of nature."

o

Outbursts. Screams. Perpetual weeping. Devout women cried in public, humiliated themselves, created scenes. In source after source, they describe tears as food. Marie d'Oignies: "These tears are my refreshment. Night and day they are my bread." They clear the way for truth, can't be ignored or gaslit away. In that sense, tears are nourishing. They confirm visions. They can be instructive.

o

Elizabeth Barrett Browning: "earth's fanatics make / Too frequently heaven's saints." How we love to read about eccentric people. How we hate to meet them in real life.

o

Not much has changed in the literary world since the first millennium BCE. What I mean is, in *Ecclesiastes* we read "Of making many books there is no end" and "Vanity of vanities, all is vanity."

○

First, they outlawed nostalgia. Then any reference to the cosmic universe, to galaxies, gravity, or stars. Birds and clouds, rivers and flowers: these are the signs of false consciousness, which you must ruthlessly pluck out. Next they forbid you to write about dreams; recounting the innocent dreams of childhood is now an unforgivable crime. Blasphemy and piety were equally forbidden. Better to avoid both belief and disbelief, they said, and walk the central path. There is danger—social danger—in having convictions. Job was a liar. Antigone an incomprehensible bore. Best not to read at all, they tell you, as they beckon you toward them. Best not to write.

○

Is it possible to write a good poem? I have my doubts. But there have been good deaths, ones with great romantic catalysts: Empedocles' volcano, Shelley's tempest. The best poem is the best death, the flower of a life most patiently endured, one of those ambiguous endings that continues, after a hundred re-readings, to produce riches.

○

On self-sufficiency. A hermit in the Egyptian desert asked an elder for advice. The elder told him: "Go and sit in your cell, and your cell will teach you everything." I think this makes for fantastic writing advice. No one can help you. Everything you need, you have.

○

Don't ever shame a person for not having read a book. In most cases, they're not yet ready for it. They might never be ready. You yourself who have read it thoroughly, have studied it and taken notes, you who may even have taught the book before, might not yet be ready.

○

Thousands have claimed to have been healed by saints' relics—a piece of flesh or cloth might cure one's blindness, a severed head eczema, a fingerbone bubonic plague. Body parts, sometimes whole corpses, humeri and femurs, skin and nails, jars of blood, all dried, or flayed, or pickled, incorruptible and therefore blessed. Francisco Franco, the fascist butcher of Spain, slept beside the bejeweled, mummified hand of St. Teresa of Ávila for decades. Upon his death, he was found clasping it. Believers have described the beauty of saints' mummies, which according to many accounts give off a sweet smell, as of flowers.

○

On self-sufficiency. Maybe the pursuit of self-sufficiency is impossible, a failure by design. As Epictetus says, "Who is really self-sufficient, fool—apart from the universe itself?"

○

There is no greater pleasure than being good at what you do. I mean this in all possible senses of that most mysterious of words in English, that *bête noire* of the spirit: do.

○

Poems, ideally, should be like saints' lives. That is, they should be experiments in magical thinking and include at least two miracles.

○

Language: the promise of infinite possibility from finite means (A—Z). Like ions and electromagnetic fields, words are charged with power. The fundamental terms of physics apply just as well to poetry: work, movement, force. And the very best poems, vectors of a numinous energy, to apply a phrase of Hart Crane's to the divine mathematics of the universe, "condense eternity."

○

Those who write at night, whether they like it or not, feed on memory. The memory of everything that happened to them during the day. And those who write early in the morning, just after waking up? They feed on dreams.

Ten Lyric Pieces

1.

Blue tunnels upward, and with it
Pink and red speak out. Men,
Never much for *idées reçues*, confused
Bees with flowers, took notes
On situations that arose from fruit.
A darling prospect this: that art
Would infect us with its bullet points
And level sights with words, but
That's what it was like, adjuncting
In the year we said we wouldn't

2.

Work. Leisure. Then nightingales
To dispute the rain with. Owls
Though usually rivals, are blinded
By each other's faults, the same as us,
Who carry ourselves with grace
While working two jobs, maybe three
If we're lucky enough to have one
Song. A ballad never written
Down by those who work, yet sing
Songs by Victorians imparadised

3.

And by us cast aside. The cathedrals
Of other centuries enchant us
With their silence. Aside from us
What people do they wait for
To enter them, to forget themselves
In entering them, the anarchic
Ones, who work, and pray, and fight
All day for nothing, those women
Who, in love, embroidered tapestries
For the Lord in the year of

4.

#MeToo. 2018. Will the world be
Better by the time you read this?
Will asphodel return in time
For spring? Myself, I think the world
Of the world, but hope to find it
Dying. We shouldn't be here, you
And I, without calendars to tell us
When to reap, sit up, ring bells
And bury peach leaves by the moon
To authenticate our experience

5.

Of love, we tread the *via negativa.*
The only path through woods
As dark as these. Like Peter Abelard
I walked all night and listened
To my own, my only, ardor steal songs
From the treetops. It's a trick
I played on nature, our landlord
Who rents to us this furnished studio
The mind is, it costs so much
To live within walking distance of

6.

The moon. Neptune. Sorrow. It began
With these three things: a theory
As to why our lives are spent
Between pleasure and brief absences
Of pain, coffee on cool mornings
With a view of the mountains
Before traveling on, between cities
On either coast, spending a day
At the museum in transit between
Centuries, epochs, eras, points in space

7.

To wander through, directionless.
Or to write a dissertation, say,
On nightshades, how they echo
Brightness back at us and drip
Water on the pages of a book
I once wrote, or wanted to write
But didn't, a Breton lay set in
An Arkansas a princess fortnightly
Summoned up to relieve herself of
Boredom, a book of poems I will

8.

Not write. Jane, it's Sara, can you
Hear me? This might not be the best
Way to communicate with you.
Are you there Jane? It's hard to read
The news. California's yet again
On fire, nothing is happening
The way we thought it would. The Bay
Is too expensive for poets, who cares
That flowers grow along the 1
All year. I'm trying to get you out
Jane. I want a better world for Opal

9.

To grow up in. It takes a lifetime
To grow up, which is another question
It takes growing up to answer:
That time you recognized the drone
Of crickets as a music worthy
Of itself alone, a work song native
To evening we learn in time to forget
The melody of. Like learning
How to police oneself in private
It gives more than we take until we

10.

Come anew.

Thank you to the editors of *Apartment*, *Berkeley Poetry Review*, *Blazing Stadium*, *The Canary*, *The Harvard Advocate*, *Hyperallergic*, *Oversound*, *Poem-a-Day* (Academy of American Poets), *Poetry*, and *The Yale Review*, where versions of these poems appeared.

Thank you to Ben Estes and Alan Felsenthal of The Song Cave. And to the brilliant Emma Steinkraus for her portrait of me, Gris-Gris, and Mr. Doodles.

Thank you, for different reasons, to Cody-Rose Clevidence, Christopher Violet Eaton, Jane Gregory, Hannah Brooks-Motl, Martin Corless-Smith, Emily Sieu Liebowitz, Elaine Kahn, Daniel Poppick, Emmett Buckley, Geoffrey G. O'Brien, and Jennifer Moxley, as well as to the Eatons/Burts and Nicholsons.

This book is in memory of Matthew Henriksen: "When you take the lost road / You find the bright feathers of morning / Laid out in proportion to snow and light."

OTHER TITLES FROM THE SONG CAVE:

1. *A Dark Dreambox of Another Kind* by **Alfred Starr Hamilton**
2. *My Enemies* by **Jane Gregory**
3. *Rude Woods* by **Nate Klug**
4. *Georges Braque and Others* by **Trevor Winkfield**
5. *The Living Method* by **Sara Nicholson**
6. *Splash State* by **Todd Colby**
7. *Essay Stanzas* by **Thomas Meyer**
8. *Illustrated Games of Patience* by **Ben Estes**
9. *Dark Green* by **Emily Hunt**
10. *Honest James* by **Christian Schlegel**
11. *M* by **Hannah Brooks-Motl**
12. *What the Lyric Is* by **Sara Nicholson**
13. *The Hermit* by **Lucy Ives**
14. *The Orchid Stories* by **Kenward Elmslie**
15. *Do Not Be a Gentleman When You Say Goodnight* by **Mitch Sisskind**
16. *HAIRDO* by **Rachel B. Glaser**
17. *Motor Maids across the Continent* by **Ron Padgett**
18. *Songs for Schizoid Siblings* by **Lionel Ziprin**
19. *Professionals of Hope: The Selected Writings of* **Subcomandante Marcos**
20. *Fort Not* by **Emily Skillings**
21. *Riddles, Etc.* by **Geoffrey Hilsabeck**
22. *CHARAS: The Improbable Dome Builders* by **Syeus Mottel** (Co-published with Pioneer Works)
23. *YEAH NO* by **Jane Gregory**
24. *Nioque of the Early-Spring* by **Francis Ponge**

25. *Smudgy and Lossy* by **John Myers**
26. *The Desert* by **Brandon Shimoda**
27. *Scardanelli* by **Friederike Mayröcker**
28. *The Alley of Fireflies and Other Stories* by **Raymond Roussel**
29. *CHANGES: Notes on Choreography* by **Merce Cunningham** (Co-published with the Merce Cunningham Trust)
30. *My Mother Laughs* by **Chantal Akerman**
31. *Earth* by **Hannah Brooks-Motl**
32. *Everything and Other Poems* by **Charles North**
33. *Paper Bells* by **Phan Nhiên Hạo**
34. *Photographs: Together & Alone* by **Karlheinz Weinberger**
35. *A Better Place Is Hard to Find* by **Aaron Fagan**
36. *Rough Song* by **Blanca Varela**
37. *In the Same Light: 200 Poems for Our Century From the Migrants & Exiles of the Tang Dynasty,* translated by **Wong May**
38. *On the Mesa: An Anthology of Bolinas Writing (50th Anniversary Edition),* edited by **Ben Estes and Joel Weishaus**
39. *Listen My Friend, This Is the Dream I Dreamed Last Night* by **Cody-Rose Clevidence**
40. *Poetries* by **Georges Schehadé**
41. *Wings in Time* by **Callie Garnett**
42. *Two Murals* by **Jesús Castillo**
43. *Punks: New & Selected Poems* by **John Keene**
44. *ABC Moonlight* by **Ben Estes**
45. *Star Lake* by **Arda Collins**
46. *The Maybe-Bird* by **Jennifer Elise Foerster**
47. *Seriously Well* by **Helge Torvund**
48. *Dereliction* by **Gabrielle Octavia Rucker**
49. *Bookworm: Conversations with* **Michael Silverblatt**